Shine Brightly
Linda Ravenscroft x

Watercolour on paper
15" x 27" aprox

"The Mystic Garden"
A place of peace and tranquility, where magic is real,
a place to relax, meditate and refresh your spirit,
Enter the mystic garden for a while, I hope you enjoy
My Art .....Blessings and light Linda.

The Mystic Garden

The Fantasy Art
Of
Linda Ravenscroft

Published by
Linda Ravenscroft 2013

Foreword

First, I must admit to a bit of name envy. After all, what mythic artist
worth their wings wouldn't want to have Ravenscroft as their given
name? Evocative isn't it? But then, so is her art.
Come. Look closer. Take your time and really study Linda's art.
Indeed, this book is a splendid opportunity to do just that.

Peer carefully past the surface tumble of her elegantly drawn images
and plunge into a world of wonder and delight.

As any artist worth studying has to, Linda has quite literally opened
her heart to you,
revealing the personal secrets that lie beneath every delicate pen line
or wash of color that she strokes into life on her canvas.
See how that particular woman, wreathed in roses, feels trapped in
a life she has no wish to live and must escape at all costs?

Listen to that whisper of a promise that the young fairy maiden,
perched on that toadstool and staring so bawdily straight at you,
has yet to fulfill.
It is clear to me that this soft dance of freshly revealed secrets acts
as the thread that binds her art into a lush tapestry of waking dreams.

Say, I've got it! Let's all change our last names to Ravenscroft and fly
then through our collective imagination as one enormous flock of
black-winged messengers bringing glad news and raucous tidings
back from the kingdom of moonlight and vine and Faerie.

Charles Vess
Abingdon, VA, USA
September 2013

For My Mother and Father who made me who I am today,
My long suffering husband John, who
made me strong enough to go on,
Daughter Ivy for being my muse and inspiration,
and all those who have been there for me over the years.

"Shine brightly and be a light in dark places"

Linda

"Freeflight"
(Freedom to Fly)

We should all try to follow our dreams....Our children only stay
with us for a short time before we have to let them go out into the world.
Like the Butterflies gently released from the hands of a beautiful faerie.
Not to be held captive or restrained, but to be allowed to fly free and take their chances in the world!
"As should all good people whose dreams give them wings".

Watercolour over ink on paper
13" x 20" aporx

"Phoenix Rising"

Much of my work is very personal, based on my own
life experiences;
The Phoenix Rising is one of them.
After many disappointments,
thinking that my art was never going to get me anywhere,
with contract disputes, worrying about my daughter,
depression and sadness
The sun finally began to shine for me again,
my work began to sell, I illustrated my first book,
and finally realised that, I can make it as an artist...
I began to look at the future with optimism and joy.
This painting was the result.
I found my **"STRENGTH"**
The Phoenix Rising is an image of hope and encouragement,
for anyone who has suffered.
The Phoenix rises from the ashes;
breaking free of all despair and sadness, never giving up,
ready to start her life anew and reminding us all
that there is always HOPE in the world.

Mixed media on paper
13" x 26" aprox

"The Marked One"
Mixed media on paper
10" x 15" aprox

Some years ago I had a tattoo. Not for vanity, but as a rite of passage,
a symbol of who I was now, an artist.
After many years of doing jobs I hated, I was now
finally doing what I had been born to do....
so, I decided to have something permanent to remind me of how far I had come
and that there was no going back, no matter what.
This painting is about a faerie who also knows who
she is; one of the wise ones her tattoos are symbols of her past, present and future.
We are both marked, and now share our love of the world we live in,
she is my guide and my art is our voice.

Watercolour over ink on paper
13" x 13"

"Amaranth"

*According to mythology, Amaranth is an
everlasting flower, one which never fades,
Like an Angel it will never die, and will
always remain beautiful and pure.*

To Dream of Peace

The Love of a Mother for her child,
a dream of a better world, one without sadness or heartache,
the child sleeps in the safety of her Mothers arms
and together they dream of peace and a better world.

Watercolour on paper
10" x 15" aprox

The Keeper of Secrets
Mixed media on paper - 14" x 22" aprox
Magic and Mystery, the Keeper of Secrets.
Tell her your darkest fears, your worries and woes,
for she is bound by a sacred oath to never tell,
she will keep your secrets safe!

"A Fragile Beauty"
Watercolour on paper - 11" x 17" aprox

How time flies, that fleeting moment, a time in your life when
you are at your most beautiful, yet so young and not able
to appreciate what you have, unitl its too late.
Like a rose, beauty is so fragile and before you know it that
moment has gone! Make the most of what you have when
you are young, celebrate your youth for it happens only once.

"The Soul Searchers"

Watercolour on paper Triptych

Some say Faeries are kindred to angels, this could be true.
I heard a tale that when God closed the gates to heaven to make sure that Lucifer
and the fallen ones could not return, a few of Gods angels were
also left behind by accident, these became earth bound, and
in order to find a purpose for their existence they became fairies,
more mischievous, than their cousins, but always caring for the natural world
around them, so it came to be that the angels take care of our souls, and the fae
take care of the natural world and all its living creatures..

There are tales which say that Butterflies are lost souls who are still trying
to find their way to heaven. In these paintings both tales merge into one fairy tale

"The Soul Searchers" are some of the forgotten fae who seek out and gently
gather these lost souls (the butterflies) and guide them towards
the Angels in Heaven so that they can rest in peace.

I like to think that All religions and beliefs can surely share some common ground.

All - Watercolour on paper, 11" x 24" aprox

Gaia,
Mother of the Earth,
protector of our world,
represented in the painting are all the precious elements of the world we live in,
the ocean, the earth, mammals, insects, fresh water, the wheat of the fields
and leaves from the green wood,
she is truly rich and plentiful, always replenishing the world around us.

""Rose Tinted"
Watercolour on paper
10" x 15" aprox

Hello my friend, what can you see"?
"Nothing", she said
"The World looks fine to me"!

View the world through rose tinted lenses,
and we only see what we want to see!
How many of us are guilty of the same?

"Rio"
A celebration of a tropical paradise.
It was mentioned to me that her face was very sad,
and I was so pleased that someone had noticed this;
the meaning behind this piece is to remind us of how beautiful
our tropical rainforests are, she is sad because she wants us to
stop destroying her paradise, her home, our home, this planet Earth.

Mixed media over ink on paper - 20" x 30" aprox

"The Marionette"

Ever felt as though your life is not your own?
"The Marionette" is about not having control over your life,
when sometimes you think that there is nothing you can do
about your situation, someone else is pulling the strings.
This painting is for anyone who wants to break free from
the control of other forces no matter what they might be!!
You CAN take control again,
and create your own destiny!

Watercolour on paper - 10" x 15" aprox

Watercolour on paper
11″ x 24″ each

WHERE THE ROSES GROW
For my parents 60th Wedding Aniversary....Love is like a garden,
take care of it through good times and bad, and it will blossom

Watercolour on paper
11" x 24" each

The roses will grow, with every year you spend together,
as you share part of each others heart, this is where
the roses grow......with the love you both share deep inside your heart.

Mixed media on paper - 14" x 23" aprox
"The Faerie Chakra"
The seven colours of the chakra, to help with meditation and the alignment of
your body and soul…. stay in tune with that Faerie magic.

"OXYGEN"

The pleasure of breathing,
the air we breath is so
precious, though we
rarely give it a second thought.

Enjoy the fresh air, on a
cool windy day, go take a
big breath and
be thankful for the life it
gives us..

Watercolour on paper
8" x 30" aprox

"Oxygen" a breath of fresh air...

THE EMERALD HEART
Watercolour on paper - 13" x 25" aprox

The Line between hope and hopelessness is a very fine one.
The Emerald Heart is a painting of hope, a dream that one
day we can live together in perfect balance and harmony,
green is the colour of healing and growth,
hence the importance of the Emerald heart.

THE QUEEN OF HEARTS

Watercolour and ink on paper 10" x 14" aprox

"The Land of Not"

I shall not worry, I will not fear, I lock
such thoughts away, this land of
contemplation is where I shall stay today!

Watercolour on paper - 11" x 15" aprox

"THE EMERGENCE OF SPRING"

Whilst Winter sleeps.....
Spring gradually begins to emerge from her hand, in the form of a tiny shoot,
the sap begins spreading slowly through her veins, thawing
out her beautiful sleeping form,
soon she will turn green and Spring will take her place!!

Watercolour on paper - 10" x 13" aprox

FLORABUNDANCE
For the love of flowers, which have a natural way to make us feel
happy and positive, this is a celebration of their beauty and fragrance.
My Daughter Ivy posed for this piece.
Watercolour and ink on paper - 11" x 20" aprox

"The Dragon Tree"
A reminder to all, that Trees are living things, strong, ancient and wild
The dragons bring this tree to life, they are one and the same - ALIVE!

Watercolour and ink on paper - 12" x 22" aprox

LIFE FORCE
The power and magic of Dragons.
Bonded together, each sharing the same life force, protecting it from harm.
If they fight and separate, their life force will be destroyed.
A reminder to mankind that we should share and be more tolerant
of each other, for we also share one life force this beautiful Earth,
like the dragons in this painting, we must remain peaceful,
if we continue to fight each other our life force will be gone forever.

Watercolour and ink on paper - 19" x 27" aprox

"First Frost"
Treading gently over the fallen leaves the first frost of winter leaves her mark.

Watercolour on paper - 9" x 15" aprox

"The Calling of Merlin"

Merlin hears Arthur calling and senses his anguish, he tries to return, but Nimue
captures Merlin and entombs him in a magical cave from which he cannot escap
The Ravens depict the demise of Arthur's Kingdom and the capture of Merlin.

Watercolour on paper - 10" x 17" aprox
(Thanks to Ian Alexander for being Merlin)

"MOONSTONES" The Enchantress
Amid standing stones of blue and grey, the Enchantress waits for the end of day.
A moon of silver strikes the sky, its light is cool and clear, echoes of the past resonate within the stones
She knows their stories, of times long gone, and cries as she hears them speak, of
warriors and battles, Kingdoms lost and found, Prayers and offerings of ancient times.
Only she knows the secrets of the Moonstones.

Ink and watercolour on paper - 11" x 22" aprox

The Daughter of Avalon"
My homage to the Goddess...

Avalon has long been known as the resting place of King Arthur, with
its connection to Glastonbury in Somerset,
the Isle of Apples, is a magical place for all who seek peace and enlightenment.
This is the Daughter of Avalon, Goddess of the Isle, keeper of the chalice well.
She represents all that is beautiful and good in this world.

Mixed Media on paper - 15" x 24" aprox

The Mask of Colours

Who is she behind the mask of colours?
Her courage is a disguise.
Her hopes and dreams can all come true
with the mask before her eyes.
Colourful and confidant, dancing through the night.
She remains unknown and unashamed until dawn's early light.
Then her colours fade and drift away,
like clouds into the sky.
Her dreams subside...her heartbeat slows
As another day draws nigh.

Linda Ravenscroft

The Mask of colours I
Watercolour and in on paper - 11" x 26" aprox

The mask of colours II
Watercolour and in on paper - 11" x 26" aprox

Millennium — The Master Plan

2000 years of life gone by,
some now extinct, though we survive.
We are the Master race.
We make the rules; we've made the moves.
But can we keep the pace?
And so a game of strategy
mankind will have to play.
With daring, stealth and superb skill,
defeat would be a bitter pill.
A new Millennium will be our prize.
The future must be saved for our
children's eyes.
And so we play our Master Plan.

It will be the legacy of MAN....

Watercolour and ink on paper - 12" x 26" aprox

Small Miracles
Tiny dew drops in a faeries hand,
hardly a miracle in itself you might think.
But without these tiny drops of water
our world would not exist.
This painting is about that "Small Miracle"
we take for granted, "Water"!
Watercolour and pencil on paper - 11"x 15" aprox

"The Vanishing"

This Faerie fading away into the background,
perhaps never to be seen again,
is a symbol of my personal sadness
for the vanishing and disappearance of our skills,
ancient beliefs and traditions.
The more apathetic we become,
manufacturing little or nothing ourselves
and relying on machinery to do things for us!!
Is truly a tragedy!
What will we be without all of our technology?
Perhaps the meek will be the ones to inherit the earth,
they are probably the only humans left
with the survival skills to do so!

Watercolour and pencil on paper - 11"x 15" aprox

"sanctuary"
Safe in the care of the Green Man,
A Place of Sanctuary...Mother Nature and
her beauty must be respected by all.

Watercolour and ink on paper - 11"x 15" aprox

"The Autumn Leaf Fairy"
Watercolour and ink on paper
11" x 15" aprox

"Winters Light"
From ancient times, Winter has always been a time of
cold and hardship , the warmth of the flame keeps ore hearths and
homes cosy and free from the darkness of Winter.

Mied media on paper - 15" x 20" aprox

"Maleficent"

Beauty can be a deceiver,
it is hard to look at a thing of beauty and even more
difficult to comprehend that there
might be something dangerous or evil within.
This painting is a reminder that, perhaps,
not all beautiful things are always what they seem to be,
and that we should be more wary.

Mixed media on paper
14" x 22" aprox

"Ritual"
For meditation and balance, we all need to make time for some spiritual healing.
Mixed media on paper - 13" x 20" aprox

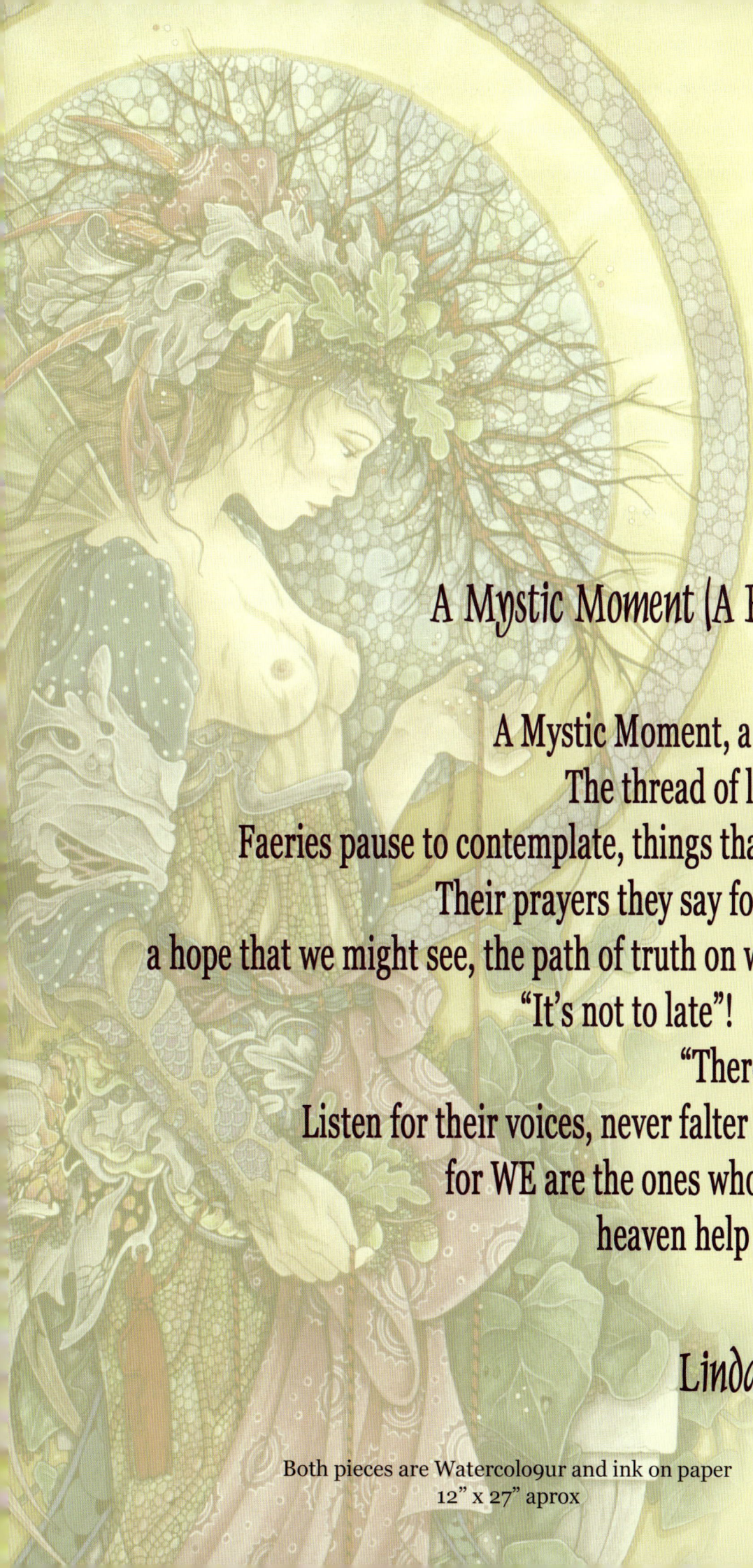

A Mystic Moment (A Faerie Prayer)

A Mystic Moment, a silent prayer.
The thread of life breaks free.
Faeries pause to contemplate, things that are yet to be.
Their prayers they say for human kind,
a hope that we might see, the path of truth on which to tread.
"It's not to late"! They whisper.
"There is still hope"!
Listen for their voices, never falter from the trail,
for WE are the ones who need to hear,
heaven help us if we fail.....

Linda Ravenscroft

Both pieces are Watercolour and ink on paper
12" x 27" aprox

"Mystic Moments I"

"Mystic Moments II"

"Golden"
Masquarade of golden light
Watercolour and ink on paper - 12" x 15" aprox

Lady of Spring (the green woman)
Watercolour and ink on paper - 11" x 15" aprox

Mixed media on paper - 20" x 30" aprox

Mixed media on peper - 15" x 20" aprox

"The Wood Wyche" and "The Oak King"

I love the ambiguity of masks,
and the secrets they can keep,
who is that person behind the mask, what can she tell u
or will she remain a secret forever?
"The Blue Mask"

Mixed media on paper – 10" x 24" aprox

"Pride"
Ink and watercolour on paper – 9" x 18" aprox

"Necromancy"
Ink and watercolour on paper – 8" x 15" aprox

"True Colours"
Mixed media on paper 14" x 24" aprox
Don't hide your feelings away, share them with someone else,
there's no need to be afraid to show your true colors, just be yourself.

"Passiflora"
The Passion flower fairy
Ink and watercolour on paper - 11" x 17" aprox

"The Owl in the oak"

The wise old owl who lived in the Oak, the more he heard the less he spoke.
The less he spoke the more he heard, why can't we all be like this wise old bird.
from my childhood - author anon.
Mixed media on paper 11" x 24" aprox

All things
Alice....

"Alice and the catterpillar"
Ball point pen and wash

"The Mad Tea Party" Pen ink and watercolour
10" x 18" aprox

Ink and watercolour on paper
11" x 11" aprox

"Daisy Chains"

Watercolour over ink
drawing on paper.

Ink and watercolour on paper
11" x 11" aprox

"Autumn Morning Fairy"
watercolour over ink
drawong on paper

Ink and watercolour on paper
11" x 11" aprox

"The Babysitter"
Watercolour over ink
drawing on paper

Ink and watercolour on paper
11" x 11" aprox

"Eye to Eye" Love at first sight,
falling in Love amongst the Sycamore leaves

Watercolour and ink on paper - 9" x 16" aprox

"Day Dreams"
Time to let your mind wonder for a while.
Watercolour and ink drawing on paper - 10" x 16" aprox

"The nothing to do fairy"
Take some time out to just sit and think for a while!

Watercolour and ink drawing on paper, 9" x 12" aprox

"Bogwood" Hidden amongst the toadstools
and gnarled tree roots, lies this beautiful Faerie.,
A reminder that beauty can be found everywhere,
even in the darkest of places.

This piece is called
"Bogwood"
named after the
goblin lurking
in the marshes.
Below is the original
pencil sketch/scribble
which inspired
this piece.

Mixed media on paper
10" x 17" aprox

"Butterfly Blue"

The butterfly was added at the very last moment to hide a
mark I accidentally made with my pen, hence the title Butterfly Blue.
Ink and watercolour on paper - 15" x 22" aprox

The Tears of Luna
The moon has looked down upon this Earth since time began;
I can only imagine the sadness it might feel as it sees our world today,
Seline, goddess of the moon cries tears for the world below and prays for its survival.
Watercolour on paper – 9" x 12" aprox

"The Snow Queen"

Wonderfully cold and icy, this is the snow queen,
White gouache has been used with a fine brush to create the fur and ice effects in this painting
Watercolour and gouache on peper - 11" x 15" aprox

"Words and Whispers"

Linda's most Inspirational images, some of her
magical work, re-designed by linda to lift the spirits
and create a more positive feeling, with the addition
of words and sentiments...
This is just a small selection from her
"Words & Whispers" collection.

"Fate"
(True colours)
Dont be afraid to show your true self, remove the mask and
follow your dreams, you can create your own destiny....
You just have to at least try.

"Inspirations" Words and whispers

"Bieleve" in yourself, you can do the
most wonderful things!

"Blessed" we are all blessed and loved.
we must never forget.

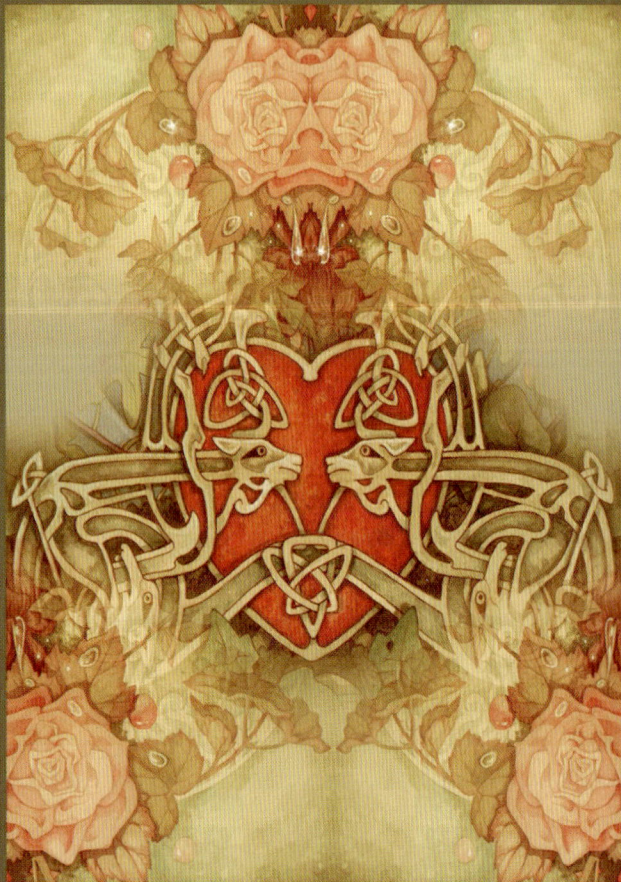

"Love" to give ones heart without
a thought for ones self

"Thankful" for all those little things we
take for granted

"Inspirations" Words and whispers

"Joy" The best feeling in the world...be joyful as often as you can.

"Shine Brightly" and always be a light for others in dark places.

"Dreams can come true" but only if you help them.

"Dance" and don't be afraid to be seen....Live for the moment.

"Inspirations" Words and whispers

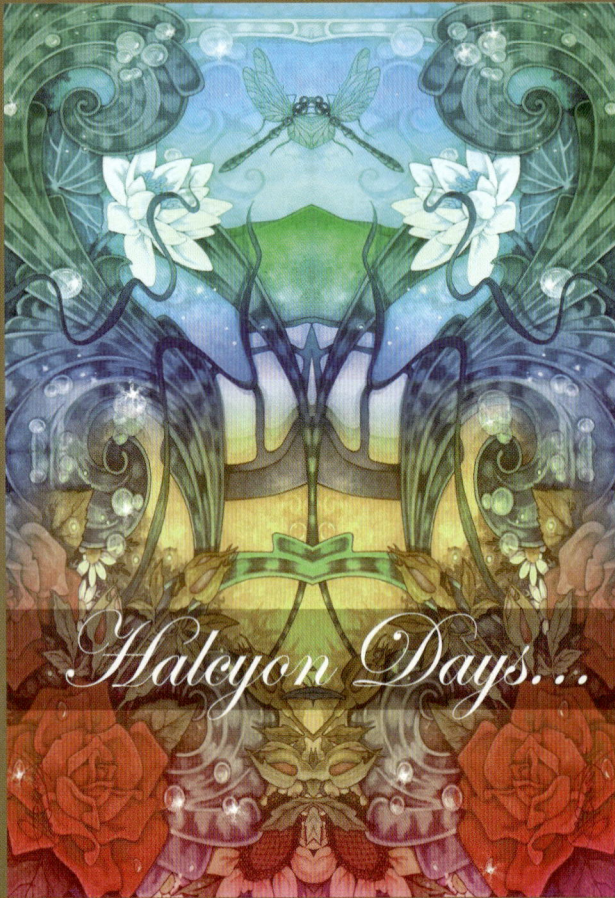

Halcyon Days...

"Halcyon days" are few and far between,
enjoy them when you can.

Go Green!

"Go Green" lets try to save the world, and
do our bit to help, no matter how small

Dark Roses.....

have hearts....

Just because something may look a little
strange, doesn't mean it 's bad.
Even dark roses have hearts.

ANGEL

Protection from harm

Death

The Devil

MYSTIC FAERIE
TAROT

LINDA RAVENSCROFT

TEXT BY BARBARA MOORE

Some of my Major
Arcana pieces
from my
Mystic Faerie Tarot

The Lovers

The Hanged Fae

The Empress

The Magician

The Fool

Tree Spirits I & II
Noble as the finest Oak, she stands amid
the trees, a spirit, a legend, a whisper on
the breeze. The truth is there for all to see.
Great sadness, when she's gone.
For the Oaks, shall weep with
the Willows when the
woodcutters axe has won... L.R.

Ink drawings with watecolour on
hot pressed paper
16" x 24" aprox

ABOUT LINDA

Born in 1963, Linda Ravenscroft is a self taught artist
who has been drawing and painting since she was very young.
Raised in the beautiful county of Cheshire, England, she lived there
with her Husband John, Daughter Ivy and animal companions for most of her life,
in 2013 she had the opportunity to follow one of her dreams, moving to the magical
town of Glastonbury, "The Isle of Avalon" in Somerset, along with husband John,
she opened her Fantasy Art Gallery "The Mystic Garden"
(named after one of her very first published pieces).

Linda became a professional artist in 1994 after her Daughter Vivien (Ivy),
was born with a serious hip defect which required years of hospital treatment
and several major operations. Linda was unable to go back to her office
job as she had planned the only other thing she thought she could
do to earn a living whilst taking care of her daughter was "Paint".

Since then her art has featured in many Fantasy/Fairy Art books, such as "The Art of Faerie"
"The World of Faerie" and "Watercolour Fairies"
Even though she had no formal art training, she has illustrated and written several
very successful Tutorial Faerie Art books, including the best selling
"How to Draw and Paint Fairies", "How to Draw and paint Fairyland" and
"The Fairy Artists Figure Drawing Bible"
She also created The magical "Mystic Faerie" Tarot Deck, and the very successful
"Woodland Faeries Calendars" produced by Llewellyn Publishing,
Her own art book "Enchanted" Faerie and Fantasy Art of Linda Ravenscroft has been a wonderful
success and is now a collectors item which is sought after all over the world.
Linda's TV appearances promoting her beautiful Card crafting C.D. ROMs, rubber stamps and other
craft materials on the Create and Craft, shopping channel here in the UK, have helped her to
become a household name not only in fantasy art circles, but as a crafter
and advocate encouraging the continuation of Hand made and crafted arts,
something which is very dear to her heart.

Linda's work is collected worldwide, in the USA and Europe in particular.
Her images can be found as counted cross stitch patterns, figurines, calendars, cards,
ceramics and giftware all over the world.
These are just a few of the wonderful things Linda has available to collectors.

Linda has been fortunate enough to be invited to many wonderful faerie and fantasy events
and gatherings all over the world where she has had to opportunity to meet many of her fans
in person and help to inspire the next generation of fantasy artists.
Opening a Gallery in Glastonbury was a dream which Linda and husband John have shared
for quite a while, an opportunity for Linda to have a place where she can work,
show her art and offer workshops to students, a chance to share some of her skills
and encourage more people to take up art as a pass time or profession.

"My inspiration comes from many sources.
I rely mostly on my dreams and inner feelings as I have done since I was a child
together with my love of nature,
and fascination for myths and ancient legends my mind is constantly visualising NEW creations.
In my view "Faerie" represents the natural world we live in, and whether you believe or not,
they do have a place in our modern day society,
in fact their light is needed more now than it ever was before.
It's time to look at this world and our feelings towards our fellow man,
and realise what harm we are doing.
Most of my images are inspirational and uplifting,
offering hope or a thought for the future of this beautiful world we live in.
I truly believe that we all have a little bit of Faerie light within our hearts,
helping us to make the right decisions
in our everyday lives we just have to look for it, and let it SHINE in the darkness"!

"Shine brightly", no matter what you do in your life, simply do the best you can, this is
your way of shining, the more of us that shine, the less darkness we will have in the world.
so
"Shine Brightly and try to live your dreams".
Linda R

Linda - photograph by Ivy Ravenscroft

Our Young Artists
CALLING UP THE COBRA

This amusing caricature of a snake charmer, complete with bed of nails and "Eastern ladies," is an entry in the Warrington Guardian Series Junior Art Competition by Linda Malam, aged 7, 62, Darwin Street, Castle, Northwich. Full details, rules and entry coupon are published in this and all editions. Closing date for entries is Thursday, March 11.

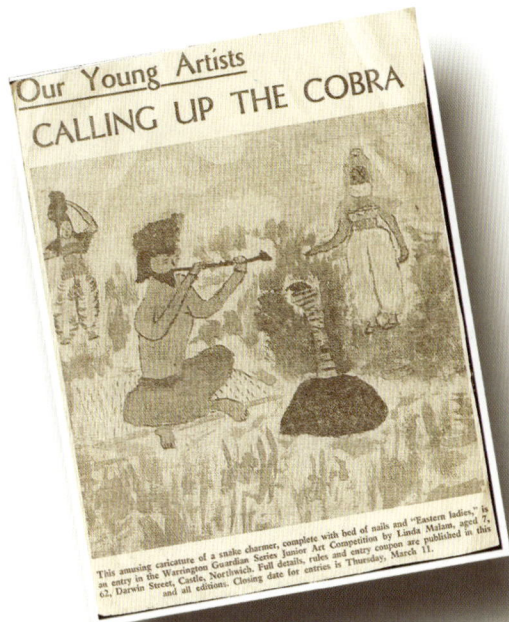

My art in the early days,
I was always drawing..
Age 7 Years..

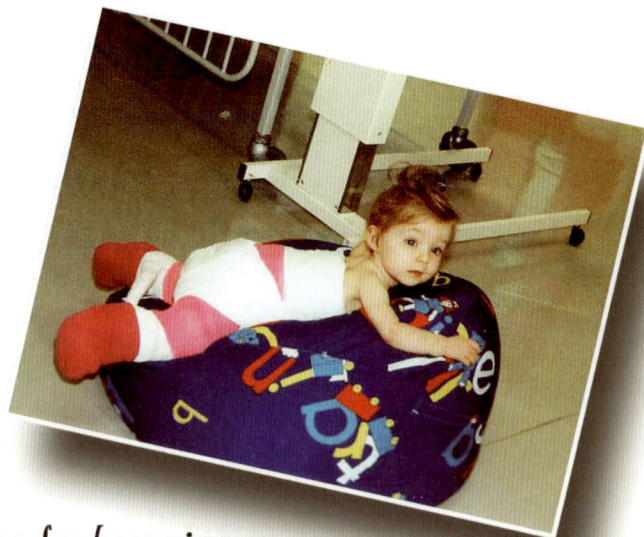

My reason for becoming an
artist...in 1993 Vivien (aka. Ivy) was born.
She was so brave.....

My wonderful, inspirational
parents...Nel and John..

I am always making things
meet my Story teller Elf...Ralph!

My first studio, built by
my Husband John and my Father...

FAIRIES
HOW TO DRAW AND PAINT

Enchanted
The Faerie and Fantasy Art of
Linda Ravenscroft

Ivy making jewellery
in the studio

Anubis our lovely
pooch..

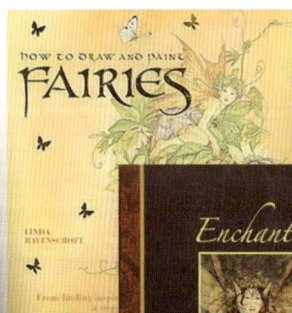

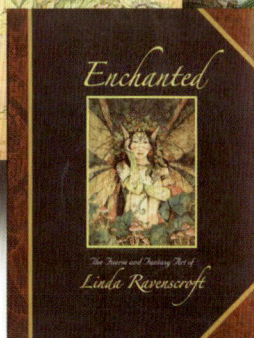

Some of my publications

Hubby John and Ivy

At the Television Studio, ready to promote my craft C.D.s...

Daughter Ivy, my muse, modelling for me...

Ivy modeling for David Webb www..d.r.photography.co.uk...

At last...My own Gallery, in the magical town of Glastonbury "The Isle of Avalon", Somerset, UK Welcome to "The Mystic Garden"....

Hints and tips

As many of you will know I have illustrated and written several successfull tutorial books about how to draw and paint faieries andfantasy subjects, and I hope that one day I have the chance to produce some more, however in the mean time, I wanted to share just a few snippets of art wisdom with you, in the hope that they will help and encourage you to pick up a pencil,brush or ball point pen and have a go yourself...

Some important pointers.

Never use cheap paper, especially if you are painting with watercolour or acrylic, always get the best quality paper you can afford, preferably 140lb in weight or above. Brushes are also important, I have a selection of cheap and expensive ones, the lower price brushes can be used for messy jobs, such as stippling with acrylic paint, and using mediums which may damage your good brushes, some acrylic or metalic paints can do this, so dont be worried too much about brushes, use your own instinct, for watercolour you can find some excellent man made fibre brushes which are almost as good a some of the natural brushes, at less cost too.
When chosing watercolour paints, try to buy artist quality paint, the colour pigments are much better and will last over time, if you cant afford artist quality, try student versions, but dont get very inexpensive paint you will just end up dissapointed.

I am often asked how do I get my work recognised?.

I see many young artists trying to copy or emmulate other artists, which is wonderful for practice, however I always point out that in order to find their own recognition, they must create their very own style. Look at all the wonderful art by all means, then, close the book behind you and ask yourself, what is it that I can do....this is what will make you stand out from the crowd....**This is what will make you, YOU!**

Keeping copies of work for the future

If you intend to use your work in the future as prints or for publication in books etc, always make sure that you keep the best copies you can. Scan the image into a compute if possible at a minimum quality of 300dpi, this is the minimum quality requirement for many book/magazine publishers and is also suitable for use in art printing.
If you are unable to scan the image yourself, there are specialist companies who can scan artwork for you. The images can then be kept on a computer disc, hard drive or other digital media.
Having your images saved like this is very important, once your original has gone, you may never get the opportunity to see the image again, the copyright remains that of the artist, (providing you didn't agree to sell the copyright - something you should never do without great consideration), therefore the artist can continue to ear a living by use the image as an art print or other licensed products.

Sketching

One of the most important things you can do as an aritst, is to keep a sketch book or two, take them with you as often as you can, and just doodle away! quite often a small thumbnail sketch can end up as a major piece of artwork.

I like to use a ball point pen for my sketching, as I always have one in my bag, they are great to use, and just need a little time and practice to get used to the technique. My sketching always keeps me busy when travelling especially by air, I hate flying so sketching takes my mind off the horror of the flight ...see my sketch book section for some of my own sketches and travel drawings.

Sketching with a ball point pen

Using diagonal sweeps, draw with the pen lightly at first, applying more pressure as you go, this will create a much darker appearance,

Apply pen strokes in all directions, not just diagonally, practice creating shading effects by applying more or less pressure to the pen.

Here the cross hatching is clearly visible. You can see that by adding more layers of hatching lines in opposite directions the image becomes darker, also, by applying more pressure to the pen the image becomes bolder still..

detail of mushrooms

First stage, sketching out the shapes, and laying down the first hints of shading using the cross hatching technique.

keep applying lines, adding more to shaded areas, creating depth and shadow. (far right - completed ink drawing - above right with watercolour wash added).

The squares on the drawing are exactly twice the size of the squares on the acetate placed over the photograph, making a larger image. Make the drawing by working on one square at a time.

USING A GRID

To try this technique you will need:-

A sheet of acetate
Sharpie, permanent marker pen –fine nib
Ruler - to make the acetate grid to apply over the photograph
This can be re-used many times for other photographs
HB Pencil for drawing and marking the grid

A grid can be a very useful tool for re-creating photographs and images.
Unlike tracing it is possible to make images larger or smaller than the original.
The only disadvantage is that you have to carefully remove the grid pattern from your drawing paper after you have completed your drawing.

Method

Using an A5 (8" x 6") aprox size piece of acetate a ruler and permanent pen mark out even 2.5cm (1inch) squares over the whole sheet.
Place the sheet over the image you want to copy and enlarge, in this case I have chosen a photograph of some foliage.
Work out how many squares cover the image, then using the
HB pencil and ruler very faintly draw out the same amount of squares onto your drawing surface,

NOTE - if you want to make the image larger make the squares bigger, for example if you wish to make the image twice the size make the squares twice as big, so 1 inch squares become 2 inch ones.
Then start to fill in one square at a time, concentrate on just that one square.
By working in this method it is possible to re-create a pretty accurate facsimile of the image.
See my sample – Although this is quite rough, it still looks quite accurate.

Removing the grid lines

I might suggest that you paint a watercolour wash over the entire image or outline it with pen, when this is dry carefully erase the faint grid lines.

THE COLOURS OF FAIRYLAND -BASIC COLOUR KNOWLEDGE

Before you begin to paint, it is important to have some basic understanding of colour and how to combine them. The ability to mix and create new shades is a skill which comes with experience and practice though if you follow a few basic rules it is possible to create a wide variety of different shades and colours with only a basic colour palette.

Colour Wheel showing secondary colours

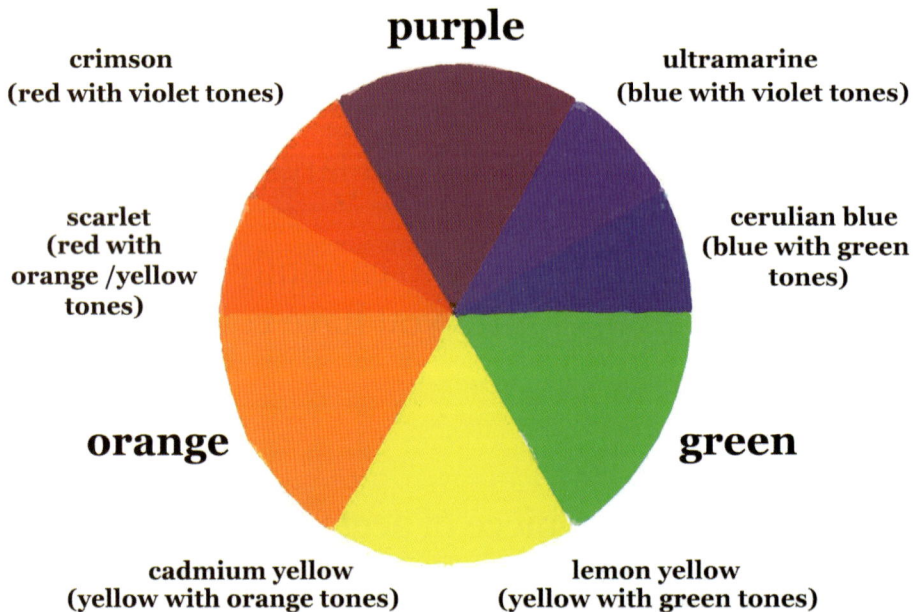

purple

crimson
(red with violet tones)

ultramarine
(blue with violet tones)

scarlet
(red with
orange /yellow
tones)

cerulian blue
(blue with green
tones)

orange

green

cadmium yellow
(yellow with orange tones)

lemon yellow
(yellow with green tones)

PRIMARY AND SECONDARY COLOURS

Most of us know that there are three main primary colours red, blue and yellow, by mixing any two of these primary colours together will make a secondary colour, orange, green or violet, however there is more than one shade of primary colour, so in order to create a successful array of colours you will need a total of 6 primary shades

Cadmium yellow (Yellow with an orange hue) warm
Lemon Yellow (Yellow with a green hue) cool
Scarlet (red with an orange/yellow hue) warm
Crimson (red with a blue/violet hue) cool
Ultramarine (blue with a violet hue) warm
Cerulean (blue with a green hue) cool

The each of these shades are primary colours though when they are mixed in the usual way they create different shades of secondary colours.

COMPLIMENTARY COLOURS

A complimentary colour is the shade directly opposite on the colour wheel, for example yellow is opposite to violet (blue / red), blue) is opposite to orange (red / yellow) and so on, each complimentary pair will consist of one primary colour and one secondary colour, complimentary colours can be used very effectively in paintings, creating very vibrant effects, for example violet and yellow pansies always look bright and invigorating.

TERTIARY COLOURS

Tertiary colours are produced when mixing a primary colour with a secondary colour, if you mix a primary colour with the secondary colour next to it, you will create a harmonious shade, for example yellow with green will make a lovely yellow green shade, however if you mix the yellow with its opposite secondary colour lilac, you are likely to get a more neutral colour such as brown. Experiment with the colours you have and try mixing them with each other, you will be surprised at how many different shades you can achieve with so few colours.

PRIMARY COLOUR MIXES

(See samples)

In order to achieve vivid colour mixes, its is a good rule of thumb to remember that if you want a bright Orange, mix together the two shades of red and yellow which contain more of that orange tone to them, that way you will mix the brightest shade. I.e. cadmium yellow and scarlet red will make a bright vivid orange, however lemon yellow and crimson will make a paler muted orange.

BASIC PALETTE

SCARLET	CRIMSON	CADMIUM YELLOW	LEMON YELLOW	YELLOW OCHRE
RAW UMBER	BURNT UMBER	RAW SIENNA	OLIVE GREEN	HOOKERS GREEN
CERULEAN BLUE	ULTRAMARINE	INPERIAL PURPLE	LAMP BLACK	CHINESE WHITE

Floral colour shades

cadmium yellow, chromium orange and ochre for crysanthemums and marigolds

scarlet red and lamp black for poppies

cobalt violet and rose majenta for mallow and roses

white, sap green and specks of cadmium yellow for delecate blossoms and flowers

pale cobalt green with olive tips and cadmium stamens for Helebore flowers

cadmium yellow for buttercups with a burnt umber centre for sunflowers

cobalt blue, ultramarine and cadmium yellow for forget-me-nots or perriwinkles

violet and ultramarine violet for spring viola flowers with lamp black centres for clematis or passionflowers

crimson red and chinese white and lamp black centres for anemones

COLOUR SHADES

Colours have temperatures according to the pigments contained in them, cadmium yellow is a warm colour because it contains an orange hue, yet lemon yellow is a cooler colour because it contains a green hue.

USEFUL BASIC PALETTE

Here is a selection of useful colours, suitable as a basic palette, it contains all 6 suitable primary shades for colour mixing along with a few extras to make things easier, the colours consist of

COLOURS OF FAIRYLAND – FOG/MIST AND SKIES

Here is a basic selection of colour schemes to help you to re-create certain weather conditions, the condition of the weather could be quite an important element in one of your paintings, for instance if you were creating a painting which requires a stormy sky, it would be a good idea for you to know exactly which colours might help you to achieve that menacing stormy appearance. Hopefully this small but useful colour palette will give you some ideas and inspiration.
All of the painted samples have been produced from a palette of just 9 colours, and by mixing and matching them together it is possible to re-create several different elemental looks.

COLOUR PALETTE ELEMENTS
This is a basic selection of colours all of which are great for creating and reproducing certain weather conditions, although some of the colours can be used alone, most of them will create a more convincing effect when at least two different colours are used together.

COLOURS OF FOG/MIST AND SKIES

NEUTRAL GREY

SEPIA

WARM GREY

PAYNES GREY

ULTRAMARINE

COBALT TURQUOISE

INK BLACK

OLIVE GREEN

ALIZARIN CRIMSON

ROLLING SEA MIST

This effect was created using washes of warm grey and olive green, the warm grey was painted at the top of the piece with olive green at the bottom, both colours merge in the centre or at what would be the horizon line, whilst the paint was still wet I lifted some colour out using a scrunched up piece of tissue. Note the brush strokes are horizontal; this helps to give the effect of the water in the foreground.

LOW LYING FOG

The castle can be seen emerging from the fog, in this sample Payne's grey wash was applied to the top and bottom of the piece with a wash of warm grey in the centre, giving a tonal look, which is dark at the top and bottom though softer in the centre, the castle towers were added after the paint had dried using the ink black, make sure there is no detail in the centre, by gradually fading the black colour making it look as though the base of the castle is hidden in the fog.

MISTY MOUNTAINS

The use of only two colours creates the atmospheric misty appearance in this small sample. Payne's grey wash at the bottom and sepia wash from the top, both blended through into the centre of the piece, whilst still wet I lifted out some of the colour using a small piece of tissue, then the painting was left to dry before using a sepia wash to add the detail of the mountain top

A STORM BREWING

Again just two colours are used for this moody sky, washed of ink black and alizarin crimson are applied in horizontal strokes in opposite corners, of the painting, allow the colours to bleed together to make the clouds, you can tissue out as much or as little of the wet paint as you wish, until you achieve your desired effect.

Step by step using salt

Try using salt sprinkled into wet watercolour washes, it creates a
very subtle but attractive effect, it looks rather like little crystals scattered throughout the paint.
In this sample I have chosen a simple little fairy figure with some toadstools.
The salt will be sprinkled freely into the paint in stages. This is a technique, which you can try
straight away with the paints in your palette;
you can adapt this idea to use the colours available to you. Simply follow the steps and see what
effects you can achieve.

0. Start by making a sketch of your fairy
using a good quality H.B. pencil.

1.   Using an Olive green colour I applied a wash
to the background creating a frame around the
fairy, whilst this was very wet I sprinkled on the salt,
this shows the salt still in place, it should be
brushed away carefully when the paint is
completely dry.

2. This shows the same olive green with the
salt brushed away; you can just see the delicate
marks left by the salt.

3. Sap green and hookers green washes were allowed to bleed into each other creating a foliage effect then the salt was sprinkled into the paint.

4. The same treatment was given to the fairies dress with a slightly darker Windsor green.

5. The wings are slightly more complicated, allowing the ultramarine and cerulean blue to bleed together I had to paint each segment of the wings separately in order to avoid the paint spreading over the whole area, sprinkling the salt in whilst the paint was wet then moving on to the next segment.

6. Having completed all of the salt effects, the painting can now be completed; a simple wash of raw umber was used for the skin tone and allowed to dry

8.
The toadstools are painted with a mixture of the
 raw umber and purple madder both colours applied
 when wet and allowed to bleed into each other.

9.
More definition is added to the painting with
a fine No1 brush and some sepia watercolour,
the hair is finished and the fairies eyes are painted
in and a little rose madder applied to the cheeks
and tip of the nose, some extra shading is painted
underneath the toadstools

10.

The sepia is mixed with some of the olive green and painted around the edges of the foliage to tidy up any scruffy areas, this same colour is used to create even more shading and depth the edges of the veins in the fairies wings are defined with this colour along with some ultramarine along the edges and wing tips.

he final touches, all of the salt has been removed and the painting has been tidied up, some
st minute shading is added just under the toadstool caps and under the fairy creating even
ore depth to the end result. Don't forget that this is just a sample of how to work a technique, you
n try this with the palette available to you, simply alter some of the colours, or simplify the method
y using only one colour for the background rather than three

Ball point
pen with watercolour
wash over - Oberon (above)

and Pierie fool - right

Morgan le fay
and
Rumplestiltskin

small sketches no larger
than A4 - 8" x 11" aprox

SKETCHBOOK

Ball point pen drawings with Watercolour wash

"Dryad" above 8" x 10" aprox

"Sisters of the moon" left 9" x 12" aprox

15" diameter circle

Ball point pen with Watercolour wash

"Titnia and Bottom"

"Titania and puck"

Sacred places

Friends and allies

Tree root homes

cosy cottage

SLOW JOE

BERTIE BOOKBODY

DIZZY BELL

RED CAP

ANNIE OAK

LITTLE MEG

WILLOW

Ball point pen - fairy family drawings
small post card size images

Above "Tree Mother"
and right "Ivy"
Ball pen sketches on the way
to the USA.

(Using A4 size sketch pad)

More ball pen sketches
my "Green Woman"
and "Whistful fairy"
created on a flight
to the USA.

"The Queen of leaves" pencil under drawing on HP watercolour paper

After applying waterclour, - 12" x 18" aprox

"December Glow"
graphite underdrawing on paper

Completed using watercolour and
coloured pencil. - 11" x 17" aprox

"Avalons Gold" Pencil under drawing

After using watercolour wash. - 9" x 13" aprox

My Jabberwocky
sketch made during
a train journey
to Cornwall

All these drawings
are in Ball point pen

Tea for two
sketch

Dragon - sketched during a trip to the USA

"Mae" above - come up and see
me sometime! and
my rag doll fairy to the right

Sketches made for myFairy
Artists Figure Drawing Bible
Pixies, Goblins and

Fairy Godmothers all drawn in ball point pen

Pencil scribbles
Character forming
ideas

Ball pen - Dryad sketch

Gnome ideas,
ball point pen

Book illustrations, ball pen with watercolur wash on paper

Published in my "How to draw and paint fairyland" book.

"Rapunzle"

Oil on canvas - 20" x 26" aprox

I have recently started to teach myself to use Oil paint.
I never stop trying new mediums and trying to improve my art...my Mother always said,
"Practice makes perfect"! you should always listen to your Muother.

"Lady of May"
Oil on canvas 20" x 26" aprox

AMETHYST

DIAMOND

PERIDOT

CITRINE

JADE

OBSIDION

LAPIS LASULI

CARNELIAN

ROSE QUARTZ

SMOKEY QUARTZ

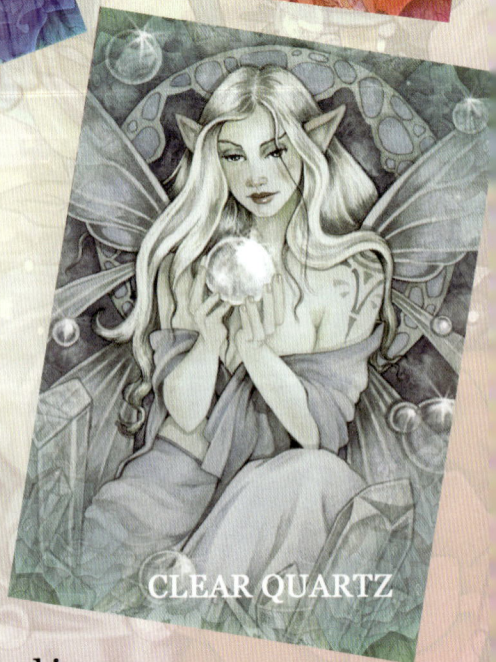

CLEAR QUARTZ

Some of Linda's 36 Faerie Gemstone Oracle card images,
Encapsulating the magic of crystals and Faerie.
Watercolour on paper - 7" x 9" aprox (each image)

The Mystic Garden
The Fantasy Art of
Linda Ravenscroft

Published by
Linda Ravenscroft 2013
www.lindaravenscroft.com

ISBN 9780992720506

Design (contents and cover): Linda Ravenscroft
linda@lindaravenscroft.com

Printed in the U.K. by: Tyson Press
Herons Way
Chester Business Park
Chester
CH4 9QR
www.tysonpress.co.uk